Shirley Priscilla Johnson's - Introduction:

Hello, thank you for purchasing this mini book. It is my hope that it will give you a little information when you are dealing with reviewers. I have been a reviewer for many years, placing hundreds of reviews on Amazon, Amazon Vine, Mid West Book review and other sites.

I have read and reviewed hundreds of books in all genres, lengths, and formats; and I have done countless interviews with agents, publishers, other reviewers, and authors. During this time I have been asked numerous questions about reviewing and decided a small book may help many.   That's how this book was born.

I believe I can relate with authors since I am one as well. I understand the intense competitiveness in the publishing world, the quest to promote your book on a shoestring, and the hopes that perhaps a great review will give you the edge you so desperately need.

Unfortunately, the art of losing oneself in a good book is slowly disappearing in our society. There are thousands of books published each year in every possible category; however, the audience for these works is getting smaller instead of larger. You as an author need every ounce of help you can get in promoting your book, and that is where we come in, reviewers. We are one more step that you can use in the promotion of your work. It is my hope that through this writing, you will have some questions answered, and better understand the world of a reviewer.

I hope you will learn some important dos and don'ts in your quest to obtain a review for your work, and that this book will bring you closer to that victory.

I have asked some of your fellow authors to submit questions to me and below I have tried to answer them as honestly as I know how. I hope you find some answers to your questions within this little book. Thank you

Shirley Priscilla Johnson

++

I'D LIKE TO KNOW: OK ASK AWAY!

+++

Questions Asked By Authors like you!

QUESTION: Just what is a review to you and how important do you think receiving a review is for the success of my book?

SHIRLEY: A review is simply one person's opinion, no more, no less. However, for a book that opinion may be the key that turns the door to success. There are several reasons for this; for one, many libraries base their purchases on reviews as do potential buyers in stores, or on-line. A good review can reveal just enough about a book to draw a buyer in like the bait on a fishhook. Buyers do read reviews.

Once the review is obtained there are countless ways to use it. For example, on your website, review sites, and it may be included in your promotional material, just to name a few. I strongly believe a review is a great plus for any book.

++

QUESTION: Do you find that reviewers read the entire book or just skim it?

No, I can't skip ahead!

SHIRLEY: Good question! I am also an author so I know how much blood, sweat and tears go into writing a book and I respect the work I am reviewing, and give it my full attention. I won't tell you that at times in some books it doesn't get boring, hearing about a pink pillow case that has no bearing on the story can cause a yawn, but I trudge on and most of the time the storyline picks up again.

Let's be honest, not every book is going to hold all people's attention, that's just how it is. Now, I can't speak for all reviewers, but I can honestly tell you that I am not a skimmer. Nor do I feel any reviewer should skim.

+++

QUESTION: Is it true that reviewers will skip over a book that is marked, "Review Copy," in favor of one that is not? Why? Does marking a review copy as such hurt the review?

FIGHTING ANGER!

SHIRLEY: Ah! I am so glad you asked this question. If there is one thing about reviewing that upsets me, this is it. I for one see RED when I receive a marked book. I consider it an insult to me for several reasons, let me explain.

First, I am not paid money to review any book. I review books because I love to read, and I hope my review will help the author in some small way. When a publisher or author marks their book immediately I feel they think my time is not valuable enough to give me their book without it being marred. Their concern for what I may do with the book after I am finished is held higher than their respect for me as a review. If they feel my time is that worthless, will they really value any review I give? I receive at least 10 or more review requests daily on my email. My time is limited as with all reviewers. I like to give it to people who respect me.

Now I understand authors or publishers may fear a reviewer will resell the book. I don't resell books but if others do, so what is the harm? Please! It takes hours for a reviewer to read a book, how much is their time worth? What do they expect reviewers to do with all the books they review?

I have reviewed close to 3,000 books and no, I do not have everyone of these books still in my possession. Yes, I have kept some, but most I have passed along.! Some to friends, who love to read. Some I have given to our local Hospital, some I have shared with churches for their children's church.. Each one found a home, except for the marked ones, they have gone to the Good Will where I hope someone will enjoy them.

I, as an author am thrilled if someone passes my book along. It's much better than sitting in the closet. They are helping to get my name out there and I say, thank you. It's free advertisement and perhaps they will seek out other book that I have written. 'Share' is my motto.

Here is a tip for you - NO charge!

If you are seeking me out for review, please DO NOT MARK YOUR BOOK....I would so appreciate it.

+++

QUESTION: How do you decide what books you will review? Do you have a choice? Do You Have Favorites?

SHIRLEY: Yes I do have a choice. All reviewers like to be queried first about a review. Most do not like books just arriving at their front door; that is a liberty that should not be taken.

However, I definitely will chose the categories' I like the most first. And there are times when I do pre-released books, where I do not have the choice of genre. I will not read PORN, or books that come against God, children, our country, or are filled with animal cruelty.

I love books on the end of time, mysteries, and light hearted books. However, I have found pleasure in many genres that I have read.

+++

QUESTION: How do you feel about the author correcting or changing your review once it is sent to them?

SHIRLEY: I do not mind if mistakes are corrected in my reviews but I do not want to see the review changed to make the book sound better than what I have written. I once had an author take my review for his book, switch some words around and send it off to review sites with my name attached. Once we found out about this, and we did find out, review sites would not take reviews of his book. The sad part is, the review I gave him was a positive one, however it wasn't good enough for him. Remember word gets out especially with the Internet now, and somehow we find out if something is done sneaky. WARNING: Cheaters never win.

+++

QUESTION: Is my book really bad if I get a terrible review?

Put up a shield!

SHIRLEY: Of course not! Put up a shield against your feelings. Different reviewers tend to like different topics more than others. Take for example another reviewer and myself. I She might love apples and I might love oranges. Her review for apples would be more positive than mine, however that doesn't mean apples aren't good. A review is ONE person's opinion; always remember that.

   You never know if a reviewer has a 'sore spot' about a certain subject and here you have a book about that subject and ask them to review it. No, that just isn't going to fly, so don't take any 'bad' review totally to heart. Learn from it, see where they are saying it was bad, sit back and make sure they aren't right. If they are, correct it, and go on. A review is just one person's opinion.

++

QUESTION: Is there something I can do to ensure a review? What makes a book 'great' for you?

Have faith in your book!

SHIRLEY: I believe every book must deliver what it promises in order to be great. If a book is supposed to be a mystery then I expect to be looking for clues, mysterious characters and the like. If it is a self-help book, I expect to come away with some useful tips. If it is a humor book, I want to have at least a few chuckles. A great book will deliver what it says it will, pure and simple.

It is important when you are finished with your book you can honestly say, that is my story and I have done

the best I can. You have accomplish what others have only dreamed about no matter what any reviewer says.

+++

QUESTION: SHOULD AUTHORS TELL THE REVIEWER ABOUT OTHER REVIEWS THEY HAVE RECEIVED, EVEN PUT A PARTIAL REVIEW IN?

SHIRLEY: Nothing makes me more angry than this. I do NOT want to know what another reviewer thought of a book. I am not that 'other' reviewer.

I suppose my strong feelings on this comes from one woman who sent me her request and had over two pages written showing me all the excellent reviews she received and how many more she was waiting for. I didn't read one of them. I cringed and quickly sent off an email telling her since she had so many wonderful reviews already I would save my review time for someone who wasn't as 'blessed' as she was.

When I receive a request and they put in "So and So gave me five stars and they said it was the greatest book they have ever read." I usually do not review the book. I don't care what so and so said about it. Believe me, I am not impressed. Why? Because I know a review is just one person's opinion. It will NOT sway me one way or another. Perhaps other reviewers don't mind, but as for me ::::: Don't put other reviews in your request. Thank you!

++

QUESTION: If you don't like the book what do you say to the author?

"Oh my!"

SHIRLEY: I usually can find some good points in every book. For example, perhaps the author writes well but the story just isn't developed. I point out the positive and work around that. I don't believe in book bashing; if I simply cannot review the book because there are no good points to point out, I will tell the author why and return it.

I have seen some new authors write some pretty lame books, but I found something good in them and as they continued to write, and of course sent me their books to review, I have seen them develop into wonderful authors. You just never know.

++

QUESTION: Do you define reviewing as different than critiquing?

SHIRLEY: Definitely! A review is a rundown of a book, the storyline, and if it delivered what it promises.

A critique is getting down to the nitty gritty and centering in on what needs improvement, what should be left in and what should be taken out. It is far more detailed and should be left to an Editor.

+++

QUESTION: Is there a 'best' time of year in which a publisher is likely to get reviews? I have heard that books with January and February pub dates have the best chance because there is limited competition.

SHIRLEY: I have heard the same thing, but to me the time of year makes no difference in the amount of books I receive or review. However, some feel a good review of a book just before the Christmas shopping rush begins might boost sales of that book better than any other time.

The problem here is that a lot of reviewers are busy with family and may not take as many books to review during this time of the year. Think about it.

+++

QUESTION: What types of promotion/descriptive materials do you find most valuable in a review copy package?

SHIRLEY: I like to have the ISBN number, page count, price, Pen name of author and illustrator, and full address of the publisher with every book that I receive. Many times the publisher's address is not inside the book and I do not like to spend time trying to find it. Other than that all I need is the book.

++

QUESTION: How soon after you receive/ read a book do you write the review? Do you let the story gel for a while? What is the longest a reviewer will take?

SHIRLEY: It all depends on how many books I have in my reading pile. However, I would say I usually get a review out within a month of receiving a book; at least I try. There have been times, however, where an author has had to wait much longer for a review. Again, it depends on the amount of books I am reviewing and the free time I have. I review the books in the order they come in once I accept the request.

I do like to let the story sit for awhile before writing my review. I mull the story over and sketch out my review in my head before I write it. I want to give the author the best and most honest review I can.

++

QUESTION: What is your philosophy on including 'spoilers' in your review?

SHIRLEY: I try very hard not to leak out information that would spoil the read for others. There have been times when authors have asked me to take something out of my review that they felt would do that; I did. I would never spoil a book's surprises on purpose.

++

QUESTION: How long does it take to read and review a book on average?

 You're reading again?

SHIRLEY: I have had some 600-page books that seem to take forever, but the average book, around 240 to 300 pages I usually finish in about two weeks, unless something happens in my home that demands my attention.

I have been known to stay up half the night reading because I have to know what happens. Of course my husband isn't always happy about it, but sometimes I just have to know how the story is going to end. Again, I let it sit a few days before I write the review.

Authors need to remember that reviewers have lives as well. We are not always able to follow a schedule in our reading and reviewing because we too have family and life to live. Be patient.

+++

QUESTION: Do you accept file attachments for reviewing a not yet released book?

SHIRLEY: I do accept pre-released books as file attachments from publishers and certain authors that I have come to know. However, I would much prefer that they be printed and sent to me, as it isn't always easy to concentrate reading a book at my computer.

+++

QUESTION: Why do some reviewers not accept eBooks?

SHIRLEY: When I first starting reviewing I did many, many eBooks, and I enjoy them. However, as I have gotten older it is much harder to sit and read at my computer. I would be happy to review an eBook if the author would like to print off a copy and send it to me. Now that Kindle and the other units used for reading have surfaced it is a lot easier to read. Even so, I am a true lover of a hard copy of any book above anything else. I myself review very few ebooks or Kindle at this time.

+++

QUESTION: Do you have specific genres you will not review?

 **NO WAY!**

SHIRLEY: Again, I will not review PORN, books against God, children or abuse to animals.

+++

QUESTION: How did you get started as a reviewer?

SHIRLEY: I love to read and came in contact with several different people who hosted review sites and asked me if I would review for them. I did that for several years, getting my feet wet, if you will. One day, my friend Laurel told me about Midwest Book Review and soon after I began to review for them. I place all my reviews on Midwest, where I am now a senior reviewer, and on Amazon, and I also review for Amazon Vine.

++

QUESTION: Why do you review?

SHIRLEY: Quite simply I love to read, learn new things, experience adventure without leaving my house, but it's more than that to me. I love to see the creativity in the different author's works. I often wonder how they came up with such amazing storylines and heartfelt words. There is a lot of talent out there and I only wish more people would open up a book and taste the wonderful meal set before them. They just don't know what they are missing.

++

QUESTION: What might make you pass on

reading and reviewing a book?

SHIRLEY: If an author is too pushy and demanding I will not read their book. The brakes come on. They simply must let me go at my own pace in order to produce a suitable review. Also, if I have reviewed a book for them in the past and they have demanded that I make changes I will not accept another book for review from them.

Understand, giving an author a review does not make us best friends, nor does it give them the liberty to nit-pick at me in other areas of my life. Believe me, that is one big turnoff, and I will steer away from any other contact with that person in the future.

QUESTION: Do publishers ask you to review books they are considering?

SHIRLEY: Yes they do, and I look at that as an honor.

+++

+++

QUESTION: Do you review everything you are asked to review? If not, what makes the difference on choosing to do the review? Interesting subject matter? Preferred genre?

SHIRLEY: I do review many of the books I get queries for, but not all. It seems the requests are getting more and more each day and I am not able to keep up with them all. We need more reviewers…How about YOU?

+++

QUESTION: What are the key things you spot in a book that helps to 'tell' you the quality of the book? For example, a great introduction, a good quality first paragraph, and a table of contents that tells you a story?

SHIRLEY: I have found a lot of great books are rather slow at the gate. I prefer a grabber at the beginning of a read, but have learned not to throw out the book just because it isn't there. You can't just pick one thing as far as I am concerned. You have to look at the whole picture, or in this case, read the whole book before coming to any conclusion. I have been bored silly at the beginning of some books and then found myself glued to the pages as the storyline moved along. It's always a surprise.

+++

QUESTION: How often do you do interviews and how can an author obtain one? May an author request an interview with you?

SHIRLEY: I do not do as many interviews as I did in the past, again because of other obligations and not enough time. However, I do think any exposure for an author is good, and certainly an interview lets people know more about you and you become more than a name.

I also love to interview publishers, for you the author, to know what they expect, and what you can expect from them. Again, time has not permitted a lot of these as late, but hopefully there will be some in the future. I don't like someone to request a interview from me only because I feel bad when I cannot do it and I know it makes the requester feel bad as well.

+++

QUESTION: Is it true that the cover of a book is important for a good first impression?

SHIRLEY: I really think a good cover is most helpful in bookstores; something that grabs the eye and won't let go. However, as far as reviewing a book I might admire a good cover, but it will have no influence on my review.

+++

QUESTION: Do you turn books down by certain publishers?

SHIRLEY: I have not as yet.

+++

QUESTION: Anything else that turns off a reviewer from wanting to review a book?

SHIRLEY: Definitely being pressured, just give us time, and being told over and over how great the book is. Also throwing other reviews in our faces that the author has received. Do not expect us to put your book above everyone else's. We are few and the demands are many. Also, don't sneak porn in the middle of the book; that makes me see red and I don't appreciate it.

+++

QUESTION: How many requests do you get for a review a month? How many do you take?

SHIRLEY: It really varies. In one day I may have as many as ten to twenty requests and have five books show up at my door that I did not ask for. I am a fast reader but do not like to put more on myself than I can handle. I wish I could tell you that I have kept everyone but that would be impossible unless I lived in a mansion, which I do not. On Amazon alone I have over 1000 book reviews and believe me I have read many more books than that in my years of reviewing. I didn't start putting the reviews on Amazon until a good while into my reviewing. I have given them away to libraries, nursing homes, relatives, friends and shut-ins, to name a few places. Please understand, this in no way reflects the quality of the books, or how much I enjoyed them. I always honor every author's book that I have accepted with my full attention and time, and I fulfill my obligation with the most honest and complete review I am capable of giving. However, I simply do not have room to house all the books I receive every year. I do have a personal library of books that have in one way or another touched my heart, have subject matter of interest to me, are written by friends, or are from authors that I simply must have every book that they write.

++

QUESTION: Do reviewers talk among themselves about books/authors?

SHIRLEY: I have from time to time talked with other reviewers. . I have been warned about troublesome authors, and been asked to review a specific book.

++

QUESTION: Should I thank a reviewer after receiving my review?

SHIRLEY: Speaking for myself, I always appreciate a simple thank you!

++

QUESTION: Do reviewers get paid?

SHIRLEY: I do not get paid for reviewing.

++

QUESTION: How much weight does a review hold to the potential reading world?

SHIRLEY: I believe it is always a plus to get your name out there anyway you can.

++

QUESTION: Does it help to build up a relationship with a certain reviewer?

SHIRLEY: I have some authors whose books I've been reviewing for years because I enjoy their writing style. I have enjoyed watching them grow and mature in their writing ability. I think reviewers need to be careful in this area; however, with the authors I have there is absolutely no problem. There have been times when I have not liked the second or third book as much as the first and I have said so. They respect my opinion, and me, and I believe use my opinions to help them grow and make the next book better. That is a healthy relationship.

+++

QUESTION: Is it a good practice to keep submitting your books to the same reviewer?

 Oh no another book???

SHIRLEY: As I have said, I have several authors that I review every new book they write. I would definitely get other reviews besides one, but to me if a reviewer keeps taking you back, they like your work, and can give you some yes and no's that you can trust. That is a good thing!

+++

QUESTION: Should you look for a reviewer that reviews in the genre you write?

SHIRLEY: I believe there is wisdom there. Take me for example; I like to review Christian works and I am always open to a Christian author. Because I am a Christian I often understand their language, perhaps, better than a non-Christian would. This can be important to an author of a certain genre; remember that.

I also love to review mysteries, children's books and young adult books. I am not a great reviewer when it comes to novels with futuristic characters. You know, Zambie from the planet Zoocan, or something like that. I have reviewed this type of book, but it is difficult for me and I often pass on them. Doing your homework in that area may well give you an edge with a reviewer.

+++

QUESTION: If you review a pre-released book, do you expect a hard copy of the book once it is published?

SHIRLEY: The author is under no obligation to send the reviewer a hard copy once it is published. I have had some authors/publishers who did and some who didn't. However, I will tell you this; I smile when one comes in the mail that I have reviewed. Receiving a hard copy after publication shows me that they appreciated my time and effort on their behalf, but it is not necessary.

+++

QUESTION: How can an unknown writer get a review from a well-known reviewer?

SHIRLEY: I have done several interviews with reviewers from different magazines and papers and asked them the same question. To be blunt they basically told me that the reading world is shrinking; therefore they simply must use the space they have for what they consider 'best-selling' works. Not something any of us authors want to hear, is it?

+++

QUESTION: If a reviewer has a published work would it be a plus to purchase their work?

You read my book?

SHIRLEY: Of course everyone wants his or her books to be purchased, but that should not be the trump card of obtaining a review from that reviewer. The review should be given freely, no strings attached. However, if they are always open to helping you with a review what a great way to say, 'thank you!'

+++

QUESTION: Once I receive my review may I use it in any way I chose?

SHIRLEY: Yes, once the review is in your hands you may use it any way your chose, as long as you do not change the content.

+++

QUESTION : I'd like to know if a reviewer could answer for me what "strong writing" means. A few agents have turned me down on my paranormal mystery because they felt "your writing isn't strong enough to stand out in today's competitive market" so does that mean my writing would be okay in a non-competitive market? I'd like to know what a reviewer looks for in a book that would classify it as "strong" or outstanding."

COME UP HERE!

How strong should I be?

SHIRLEY: I have to say that any book that I think about days, weeks or even months after I finish the read would classify as a strong work. I have read some books where the characters became so alive in my mind's eye that I caught myself wondering how they were doing. Crazy, but true! Now that's a great writer, don't you think?

++

The Final Question: The Final Word: What is the most difficult challenge for a reviewer?

SHIRLEY: I suppose first it would be turning away an author simply because there are not enough hours in the day to accept their book. Also, a reviewer has to be careful that reviewing does not become like homework. By this I mean that it becomes a burden and overtakes your life, leaving you with little time for anything else.

Always remember we volunteer to do this and we, like you, have family and other obligations in our lives. As much as we love to read and want to help authors along the way, we simply cannot justify cutting out quality time with our own families to take on two or three more review books for hungry authors. It just would not be fair. Definitely one challenge is learning the right pace in reviewing. It can be a shackle if you let it.

It takes time to write a review. I do not sit at the keyboard and just type anything. I try very hard to draw out the good points of a book and put them in the review; grabbers that will catch the attention of the one reading the review. Sometimes that is easy, other times it is hard. I will write the review and let it sit and then go back and look at it, perhaps add or take out something and finally send it off.

To me, writing a review is like writing a very tiny novel, and I do mean tiny. I want to capture the heart of the book in my review and give it to the reader. I know I have done that when an author writes me and tells me they sat in tears after reading my review, because I had found the very essence of what their book was about. That makes me smile and I know I have done their book justice.

People ask me over and over again, do all the books I read keep my attention. The answer is no! I have had some books that to me were so boring I had to make myself finish them. The sad part is that some of these books were on *The New York Times* best selling list. I wondered why!

On the other side of the coin, I have read and reviewed countless books by unknown authors that I have to tell you, if they were a movie I would have stood up and cheered. Yet , sadly, they remain in the shadow of the famous authors and may never receive the recognition they so deserve. That is heartbreaking to me, and I pray that perhaps my review will give them some encouragement to keep going and use the talent God has given them.

Understand, not every book I read is great, but I realize that perhaps to another reader the same book would be exciting. We are all different. However, almost every book has at least one good point and I do my best to dig that out and center my review on it.

Recently I read a story where the main character's actions left me very disturbed. It was particularly hard because it was a Christian book focusing on forgiveness. Even though the happenings in the story were unsettling, the author was a good writer. Despite my uneasiness with the contents of the book, their writing style was excellent, so I played upon that point. I did mention that I wasn't thrilled with the story itself, but applauded the author's writing ability. Another time I was asked to review a book about an after death experience from a young man who died after overdosing on drugs. He tagged it as a Christian genre. I have to say I love reading books such as this; however this book totally went against Christian beliefs, and I stated that in my review. I thought I was going to be buried alive for my opinion.

The author was horrified and bluntly told me that I was ruining his chances for any Christians to buy his book and he wanted me to change the review. Did I? No! If you are going to peddle a book revolving around a certain faith, or subject matter, and claim it as truth, than you better check up on what that truth is. I am not saying he didn't have his experience and I stated that in my review; however, his experience certainly did not coincide with Christian beliefs of the afterlife, and I had to make that clear. The review stayed as written; that was my final decision.

I have also been asked why I give most of my reviews on Amazon a five-star rating. That is pretty simple to explain. I try to read and review books of interest to me. Usually they are worth a five-star, but occasionally I do a four. I also feel that the author deserves some credit for writing the book at all. I have truly been blessed to read and review what I think were some great books. There is a lot of talent out there and being a reviewer has allowed me to taste the wonders of the world through their words and peek into the minds of the writers I review. I enjoy seeing how they weave endless stories that capture my heart. It is most times a true pleasure and always an adventure.

I'd like to give some advice to you. Never stop the words from flowing out from within you, because there are those of us that feast on the meals you provide. You write because you simply must quench that burning inside and if you touch but one person with your words remember, you have accomplished what most never dreamed possible. Keep going; you never know when you will finally reach your star.

THANK YOU

I would like to thank all the authors and publishers that sent their questions for use . I are sure there are still some unanswered questions out there, but perhaps that is another book in the making. I truly hope you go away with more knowledge and understanding concerning the reviewing world, and I wish you the best in your writing endeavors.

SEE YOU IN THE DREAMS YOU WRITE!

Shirley Priscilla Johnson

ABOUT THE AUTHOR

Shirley Priscilla Johnson is a senior reviewer for Mid West Book Review. She also reviews for Amazon and Amazon Vine.

She is the author of over sixty books that can be found on Amazon.com. She is also a song writer with over 3,000 songs to her credit and a retired Preacher. She is married to Robert Johnson, for 34 years, and they live in the state of, Florida.

You may go to her website to see her work at:

www.jesusinsong.com

Want to email her:

shirleypriscilla.johnson@gmail.com

God bless you all!

www.ingramcontent.com/pod-product-compliance
Lightning Source LLC
Chambersburg PA
CBHW071552170526
45166CB00004B/1653